NAME YOUR EMOTIONS

SOMETIMES I FEEL JEALOUS

Nicole A. Mansfield

a Capstone company — publishers for children

Raintree is an imprint of Capstone Global Library Limited, a company incorporated in England and Wales having its registered office at 264 Banbury Road, Oxford, OX2 7DY – Registered company number: 6695582

www.raintree.co.uk
myorders@raintree.co.uk

Hardback edition © Capstone Global Library Limited 2023
Paperback edition © Capstone Global Library Limited 2024
The moral rights of the proprietor have been asserted.

All rights reserved. No part of this publication may be reproduced in any form or by any means (including photocopying or storing it in any medium by electronic means and whether or not transiently or incidentally to some other use of this publication) without the written permission of the copyright owner, except in accordance with the provisions of the Copyright, Designs and Patents Act 1988 or under the terms of a licence issued by the Copyright Licensing Agency, 5th Floor, Shackleton House, 4 Battle Bridge Lane, London SE1 2HX (www.cla.co.uk). Applications for the copyright owner's written permission should be addressed to the publisher.

Edited by Erika L. Shores
Designed by Dina Her
Media research by Jo Miller
Original illustrations © Capstone Global Library Limited 2023
Originated by Capstone Global Library Ltd
Production by Tori Abraham
Printed and bound in India

978 1 3982 3912 8 (hardback)
978 1 3982 3911 1 (paperback)

British Library Cataloguing in Publication Data
A full catalogue record for this book is available from the British Library.

Acknowledgements
We would like to thank the following for permission to reproduce photographs:
Shutterstock: Dragon Images, 5, fizkes, 7, 11, Khosro, 17, kwanchai.c, Cover, Motortion Films, 21, New Africa, 13, pixelheadphoto digitalskillet, 10, Robert Kneschke, 19, Suzanne Tucker, 9, Veja, 18, wee dezign, 15

All the internet addresses (URLs) given in this book were valid at the time of going to press. However, due to the dynamic nature of the internet, some addresses may have changed, or sites may have changed or ceased to exist since publication. While the author and publisher regret any inconvenience this may cause readers, no responsibility for any such changes can be accepted by either the author or the publisher.

CONTENTS

What is jealousy? 4

What does it feel
like to be jealous? 6

Using your senses 8

Talking about your feelings 10

Understanding jealousy 12

Coping with feelings 16

    Mindfulness activity 20

    Glossary 22

    Find out more 23

    Index 24

    About the author 24

Words in **bold** are in the glossary.

WHAT IS JEALOUSY?

Your cousins have come to visit. They have brought their brand-new tablets with them. Yours is old and cracked. You've lost the charger. You wish you had a shiny, new tablet.

You might be feeling jealous. Jealousy is an **emotion**, or feeling. Being jealous might make you feel bad inside. But everyone feels jealous sometimes.

WHAT DOES IT FEEL LIKE TO BE JEALOUS?

Think of a time when you felt jealous. Maybe someone else won a prize in your class. Or your little brother got to pick his favourite film to watch. How did you feel?

When you are jealous, you might want to cry. Your stomach feels sore. Your ears might get hot. You may feel like shouting at the person who got what you wanted.

USING YOUR SENSES

Your **senses** can make you feel a lot of different things. We all have five senses. We hear, see and smell things. We taste and touch things too.

Seeing someone get what you wanted might make you jealous. Hearing others clap and cheer for someone else can cause jealous feelings too.

TALKING ABOUT YOUR FEELINGS

Talking about how you feel is a good thing to do. If you feel jealous, tell a family member or a teacher. They can help. You will feel better after you talk it through.

Using your words to describe your feelings may be hard at first. But don't stop trying. Use your words to tell people on the outside how you are feeling on the inside.

UNDERSTANDING JEALOUSY

You have probably been jealous of someone before. Why did you feel jealous? Did they get more **attention** than you did from someone you love?

It helps to know what happened to make you feel jealous. It helps to talk about it with someone else. You can get the jealous feelings out. Then you can let new happy feelings in.

When you are jealous, you might not want to play with your friends. You might not want to try new games. You might be afraid you'll lose. Maybe you feel like what you can do is not as good as someone else. But what you can do is just right!

COPING WITH FEELINGS

Learning how to cope with your feelings is important. It is OK to feel jealous once in a while. But don't stay jealous for long. You don't want to miss out on friendships because of jealousy.

You can learn to cope with jealousy. First, take a deep breath. Then let it out slowly. Think about something you know you do well. Remember jealous feelings will pass.

You can help others when they feel jealous. Tell them to stop and breathe in and out slowly. Help them talk about all the things that they do well.

By helping others, you can also feel **proud** of yourself. Smile at people. Cheer for them. Jealous feelings can melt away when you help other people.

MINDFULNESS ACTIVITY

You can learn to cheer for yourself. It will help you get rid of jealous feelings fast.

What you do:

1. Stand in front of a mirror. Close your eyes and take a deep breath.

2. Let the breath out of your mouth very slowly.

3. Think of three things you are good at doing. Are you good at running, drawing or baking? Maybe you are good at cheering up a friend.

4. Smile at yourself in the mirror. Say out loud the three things you do well.

GLOSSARY

attention notice, interest or awareness

emotion strong feeling; people have and show emotions such as happiness, sadness, fear, anger and jealousy

proud feeling pleased and happy about something or someone

sense way of knowing about your surroundings; hearing, smell, touch, taste and sight are the five senses

FIND OUT MORE

BOOKS

Let Go of Jealousy (Kids Can Cope), Gill Hasson (Franklin Watts, 2021)

Sometimes: A Book of Feelings, Stephanie Stansbie (Little Tiger Press, 2022)

WEBSITES

www.bbc.co.uk/bitesize/clips/zw676sg
This BBC Bitesize video shows how you can be happy at home and with your friends.

www.bbc.co.uk/cbeebies/watch/love-to-learn-jealousy
Watch this video about jealousy.

INDEX

afraid 14
attention 12
breathing 16, 18
cheering 8, 19
crying 6
emotions 4
feeling ill 6

friendship 14, 16
helping others 18, 19
losing 14
senses 8
shouting 6
talking 10, 11, 12, 18
winning 6

ABOUT THE AUTHOR

Nicole A. Mansfield is passionate about writing books for children. She loves to exercise and to sing at church. She lives with her husband and three children in Georgia, USA.